A Quick Word with

BETH
MOORE

A Quick Word with Beth Moore:
Quotations from *Praying God's Word*
Copyright © 2009 by Beth Moore
All Rights Reserved

ISBN 978-0-8054-3280-0
B&H Publishing Group
Nashville, Tennessee
www.BHPublishingGroup.com

Printed in Singapore
1 2 3 4 5 6 7 12 11 10 09

A Quick Word with

BETH
MOORE

Scriptures & Quotations from
PRAYING
GOD'S WORD

I will give them
a heart to know Me,
that I am the Lord. They
will be My people, and I
will be their God because
they will return to Me
with all their heart.

Jeremiah 24:7

Believe it or not,
the ultimate goal God
has for us is not power
but personal intimacy
with Him. Yes, He wants
to bring us healing, but
more than anything,
He wants us to know
our Healer.

Since we have the
same spirit of faith in
accordance with what
is written, "I believed,
therefore I spoke,"
we also believe, and
therefore speak.

2 Corinthians 4:13

When you speak
God's Word out loud
with confidence in Him
rather than in your own
ability to believe, you are
breathing faith. Believing
and speaking the truth
of God's Word is like
receiving blessed CPR
from the Holy Spirit.

All of you clothe
yourselves with humility
toward one another,
because "God resists the
proud, but gives grace
to the humble."

1 Peter 5:5

What blessed relief
comes when we fall on
our knees and realize
what a heavy weight pride
has been. It is exhausting
to insist on thinking so
highly of ourselves with
such mounting evidence
to the contrary!

What makes everything clear is light. Therefore it is said: "Get up, sleeper, and rise up from the dead, and the Messiah will shine on you."

Ephesians 5:14

Much of the shame we experience is wrapped up in the secret. In fact, the enemy knows that once we expose the secret places of our lives to the light of God's Word, we're on our way to freedom.

Let me experience
Your faithful love in
the morning, for I trust
in You. Reveal to me
the way I should go,
because I long
for You.

Psalm 143:8

We are not wrong to think we desperately need to be loved. We do! But we are wrong to think we can make anyone love us the way we need to be loved. Our need does not constitute anyone else's call but God's.

Christ has
liberated us into
freedom. Therefore
stand firm and don't
submit again to a
yoke of slavery.

Galatians 5:1

It is most definitely God's will for us to be free from all areas of bondage. He may not always will for us to be physically healed or tangibly prosperous, but He always wills for us to be free from strongholds.

Go, eat your bread
with pleasure, and drink
your wine with a cheerful
heart, for God has already
accepted your works.

Ecclesiastes 9:7

Jesus is incapable of suddenly deciding He no longer wants you. If you have received God's Son as your Savior, nothing you can do will cause Him to reject you. He happens to think you're worth loving. And keeping.

As for his allowance,
a regular allowance was
given to him . . . a portion
for each day until the day
of his death, for the
rest of his life.

Jeremiah 52:34

Few things beyond our salvation are "once and for all." If God teaches us victory in Christ Jesus day by day, we live in the constant awareness of His greatness and sufficiency.

You hide them in
the protection of Your
presence; You conceal
them in a shelter from
the schemes of men,
from quarrelsome
tongues.

Psalm 31:20

What a relief to
know that we'll never
battle anything that's out
of God's jurisdiction.
He can as easily defeat
His opposition on Mt.
Carmel as Mt. Zion.
It's all His turf.

Jesus replied to them,
"The healthy don't need
a doctor, but the sick do.
I have not come to call
the righteous, but sinners
to repentance."

Luke 5:31–32

Never in all of Scripture
does Christ resist the
repentant sinner. Yes,
He resisted the proud
and the self-righteous
religious, but never the
humble and repentant.
Indeed, forgiveness
is why He came.

The weapons of our
warfare are not fleshly,
but are powerful through
God for the demolition
of strongholds.

2 Corinthians 10:4

What is more
powerful than two
sticks of dynamite placed
in separate locations?
Two strapped together.
That's what praying God's
Word is—strapping them
together and igniting
them with faith in what
God says He can do.

The Lord is the One
who will go before you.
He will be with you;
He will not leave you or
forsake you. Do not be
afraid or discouraged.

Deuteronomy 31:8

We live in fear
of that which we are
certain we can't survive.
But as children of God,
we are only as fragile as
our unwillingness to
turn and hide our
face in Him.

We who live are
always given over to
death because of Jesus,
so that Jesus' life may
also be revealed in
our mortal flesh.

2 Corinthians 4:11

The longer I've walked
with God in prayer and
His Word, the less I want
Him to let me off easy.
A believer's willingness
to "do the hard thing" is
what sets him or her apart
for the extraordinary
in Christ.

If we say, "We have fellowship with Him," and walk in darkness, we are lying and are not practicing the truth.

1 John 1:6

Believers are people of
light, but sometimes the
darkness around us can be
so oppressive that we feel
it. Yet our willingness to
fellowship with God in
the midst of our difficulty
will usher forth the rays
of His wonderful light.

Flee from youthful
passions, and pursue
righteousness, faith, love,
and peace, along with
those who call on
the Lord from a
pure heart.

2 Timothy 2:22

God is not expecting
unblemished perfection.
He is looking for hearts in
constant pursuit of Him
and His righteousness.
Long-term victory results
from many short-term
victories that finally
collide, forming
new habits.

I do not trust in
my bow, and my sword
does not bring me victory.
But You give us victory
over our foes and let
those who hate us
be disgraced.

Psalm 44:6—7

Being successful describes
how we handle relatively
manageable challenges
that an unbeliever could
manage just as well. Being
victorious describes how
we live as overcomers in
the midst of Goliath
opposition.

See, today I have
set you over nations
and kingdoms to uproot
and tear down, to destroy
and demolish, to build
and plant.

Jeremiah 1:10

Strongholds can't
be swept away with a
spiritual broom. We
can't fuss at them and
make them flee. We can't
ignore them until they
disappear. Strongholds
are broken one way only:
they have to be totally
demolished.

We always pray for
you that our God will
consider you worthy of
His calling, and will, by
His power, fulfill every
desire for goodness and
the work of faith.

2 Thessalonians 1:11

Prayer keeps us in
constant communion
with God, which is
the goal of our entire
believing lives. Without
a doubt, prayerless lives
are powerless lives, and
prayerful lives are
powerful lives.

The instruction
of the Lord is perfect,
reviving the soul; the
testimony of the Lord is
trustworthy, making the
inexperienced wise.

Psalm 19:7

God may use many
different elements to
usher you to freedom, but
one thing I believe with
all my heart: the Word of
God will be the absolute
common denominator in
all genuine deliverance
from captivity.

Do not despise the
Lord's instruction, my
son, and do not loathe
His discipline; for the
Lord disciplines the one
He loves, just as a father,
the son he delights in.

Proverbs 3:11—12

One sobering thing
about the faithfulness
of God is that He keeps
His promises, even when
they are promises of
judgment and
discipline.

Whoever drinks from
the water that I will give
him will never get thirsty
again—ever! In fact, the
water I will give him will
become a well of water
springing up within him
for eternal life.

John 4:14

Why does God allow
us to spend so much of
life in the heat of battle?
Because He never meant
for us to sip His Spirit
like a proper cup of tea.
He meant for us to hold
our sweating heads over
the fountain and lap
up His life with an
unquenchable thirst.

When you pray, go
into your private room,
shut your door, and pray
to your Father who is in
secret. And your Father
who sees in secret will
reward you.

Matthew 6:6

I am convinced that
God would rather hear
our honest pleas for more
of what we lack than a
host of pious platitudes
from an unbelieving
heart.

Everything that belongs
to the world—the lust
of the flesh, the lust of
the eyes, and the pride
in one's lifestyle—is not
from the Father, but
is from the world.

1 John 2:15–16

Let's not fool ourselves into thinking that pride is a problem only for the lost. The most effective means the enemy has to keep believers from being full of the Spirit is to keep us full of ourselves.

We have renounced
shameful secret things,
not walking in deceit or
distorting God's message,
but in God's sight we
commend ourselves to
every person's conscience
by an open display
of the truth.

2 Corinthians 4:2

All we have to do
to locate Satan in any
situation is to look for the
lie. How do we recognize
a lie? Anything we are
believing or acting on that
is contrary to what the
truth of God's Word
says about us is a lie.

God is not
a man who lies,
or a son of man who
changes His mind.
Does He speak and
not act, or promise
and not fulfill?

Numbers 23:19

God's faithfulness
cannot be fathomed by
comparing Him to the
noblest of men. He does
not simply resist ignoble
tendencies. He lacks them
altogether. You can take
Him at His Word.

Lord, because of
these promises people
live, and in all of them is
the life of my spirit as
well; You have restored
me to health and
let me live.

Isaiah 38:16

I am convinced
our hearts are not
healthy until they have
been satisfied by the only
completely healthy love
that exists: the love of
God Himself.

We have come
to know and to believe
the love that God has for
us. God is love, and the
one who remains in love
remains in God, and
God remains in him.

1 John 4:16

Believe even when
you do not feel. Know
even when you do not see.
He gave the life of His
Son to demonstrate His
love. The time has
come to believe.

A thief comes only
to steal and to kill and
to destroy. I have come
that they may have
life and have it in
abundance.

John 10:10

You were never
meant to get through
life by the skin of your
teeth. You were meant
to flourish in the love
and acceptance of
Almighty Jehovah.

David said to the
Philistine, "You come
against me with a dagger,
spear, and sword, but I
come against you in the
name of the Lord of
Hosts, the God of
Israel's armies."

1 Samuel 17:45

Overcoming addiction
may be the battle of
your life. But it will also
be the most rewarding,
liberating victory of your
life. It will be your own
Goliath story for the
rest of your days.

Although these have
a reputation of wisdom
by promoting ascetic
practices, humility, and
severe treatment of the
body, they are not of any
value against fleshly
indulgence.

Colossians 2:23

If man could truly subdue all his fleshly appetites by the pure power of his own determination, he would simply worship his own will. But if the Word of God is about anything at all, it is about God's will rather than ours.

Therefore dear
friends, since we have
such promises, we should
wash ourselves clean from
every impurity of the
flesh and spirit, making
our sanctification
complete in the
fear of God.

2 Corinthians 7:1

When we approach God
in genuine repentance,
taking full responsibility
for our sins, our prison
doors swing open.
But we could sit right
there in our prison cells in
torment if we don't stand
on God's promises and
walk forward in truth.

It is I who sweep
away your transgressions
for My own sake and
remember your sins
no more.

Isaiah 43:25

Those who walk closely with God frustrate the efforts of the accuser. By the time he arrives in the heavenlies to register his accusations, God can say with pleasure, "I have no memory of that sin."

"For I know the
plans I have for you,"
declares the Lord, "plans
to prosper you and not to
harm you, plans to give
you hope and a future.
Then you will call upon
me and come and pray
to me, and I will
listen to you."

Jeremiah 29:11–12 NIV

Please know that God has a plan for you, a plan to give you a hope and a future. Satan also has a plan for you, a plan to give you hopelessness and to steal your future. The quality of your life hangs in the balance, and only you can decide.

Just as you have always obeyed, not only in my presence, but now even more in my absence, work out your own salvation with fear and trembling. For it is God who is working in you, enabling you both to will and to act for His good purpose.

Philippians 2:12–13

I'm beginning to learn to say, "Lord, my flesh is so resistant to what You want right now, but don't stop! Insist upon my best! Insist upon Your glory! Take me to the line on this, God. Don't let up on me until we've gone every inch of the distance."

Put on heartfelt
compassion, kindness,
humility, gentleness, and
patience, accepting one
another and forgiving
one another if anyone
has a complaint against
another. Just as the Lord
has forgiven you, so also
you must forgive.

Colossians 3:12–13

Forgiveness is not
defined by a feeling,
though it will ultimately
change our feelings. It is
the ongoing act by which
we agree with God over a
matter, practice the mercy
He's extended to us, then
surrender the situation
and the hurtful person
to Him.

Why am I so
depressed? Why this
turmoil within me?
Put your hope in God,
for I will still praise
Him, my Savior
and my God.

Psalm 42:5

Take heart!
Men and women
of the faith far more
godly and effective than
I will ever be have fought
depression. Remember,
the defeat is not in
fighting depression
but in giving in.

In all their suffering,
He suffered, and the
Angel of His Presence
saved them. He redeemed
them because of His love
and compassion; He
lifted them up and
carried them all
the days of
the past.

Isaiah 63:9

God sees our suffering
and knows the depth of
our need. He anguishes,
yet He waits until the
tears that have fallen on
dry ground or upon the
shoulders of others
equally frail are poured
instead before His
throne.

"Let us discuss this,"
says the Lord. "Though
your sins are like scarlet,
they will be as white as
snow; though they are as
red as crimson, they
will be like wool."

Isaiah 1:18

God loves you with all
His heart. With His Son's
life, He has already done
everything necessary to
set you free. Now He just
wants you to let Him
apply it to your life.

Simon, Simon,
look out! Satan has
asked to sift you like
wheat. But I have prayed
for you that your faith
may not fail. And you,
when you have turned
back, strengthen
your brothers.

Luke 22:31–32

As much as I wish
my testimony could
be "defeat followed
by salvation followed by
consistent victory," it isn't.
It is "salvation, confusion,
misery, defeat, success,
more defeat, unmitigated
failure, then victory." My
testimony is that there
is life after failure.

You are from God,
little children, and you
have conquered them,
because the One who is
in you is greater than
the one who is in
the world.

1 John 4:4

I have a long way to go,
but I have put the devil
on alert: he may make my
life very difficult but he
cannot make me quit. For
I, like you, am one of
God's dear children.

Therefore, submit
to God. But resist the
Devil, and he will flee
from you. Draw near
to God, and He will
draw near to you.

James 4:7–8

It is never the will
of God for warfare to
become our focus. The
fastest way to lose our
balance in warfare is to
rebuke the devil more
than we relate to God.

Do not be
conformed to this age,
but be transformed by
the renewing of your
mind, so that you may
discern what is the good,
pleasing, and perfect
will of God.

Romans 12:2

In praying Scripture,
I not only find myself in
intimate communication
with God, but my mind is
being retrained, renewed,
to think His thoughts
about my situation
rather than mine.

Indeed, it was
for my own welfare
that I had such great
bitterness; but Your love
has delivered me from the
Pit of destruction, for
You have thrown all
my sins behind
Your back.

Isaiah 38:17

Deliverance

Freedom rarely comes
to a person who does not
get intimately involved
with God for himself or
herself. God is far more
interested in our getting
to know the Deliverer
than our being
delivered.

Dear friends, if our
hearts do not condemn
us we have confidence
before God, and can
receive whatever we ask
from Him because we
keep His commands and
do what is pleasing
in His sight.

1 John 3:21–22

I often ask God to keep me balanced in the whole counsel of His Word and to help me discern when I'm getting off track. I may be at war with a powerful, unseen enemy, but I can be at peace with the Lord God omnipotent!

Jesus said to him,
"'If You can?' Everything
is possible to the one who
believes." Immediately
the father of the boy cried
out, "I do believe! Help
my unbelief."

Mark 9:23–24

Believe God can do
what He says He can do.
Believe you can do what
He says you can do.
Believe God is who He
says He is. And believe
you are who He says
you are.

Therefore we will
not be afraid, though the
earth trembles and the
mountains topple into the
depths of the seas, though
its waters roar and foam
and the mountains quake
with its turmoil.

Psalm 46:2–3

Faith is not
believing in my own
unshakable belief.
Faith is believing an
unshakable God
when everything in
me trembles
and quakes.

I will break down
your strong pride. I will
make your sky like iron
and your land like bronze,
and your strength will be
used up for nothing.
Your land will not yield
its produce, and the trees
of the land will not
bear their fruit.

Leviticus 26:19–20

My name is Pride.
I am a cheater. You like
me because you think I'm
always looking out for
you. Untrue. I'm looking
to make a fool of you.
God has so much for you,
I admit, but don't worry.
If you stick with me,
you'll never know.

Surely You desire
integrity in the inner
self, and You teach me
wisdom deep within.
Purify me with hyssop,
and I will be clean;
wash me, and I will be
whiter than snow.

Psalm 51:6—7

If we're going to live
in freedom, we have no
choice but to renounce
every single secret place
of sin to God, exposing
even the smallest detail to
the light of God's Word.
This is the means by
which God injects truth
in the inner parts.

The Lord will
not reject us forever.
Even if He causes
suffering, He will show
compassion according
to His abundant,
faithful love. For He
does not enjoy bringing
affliction or suffering
on mankind.

Lamentations 3:31—33

Throughout life we will lose people who really loved us to death or to changing circumstances. As dear and rich as their love was to us, it was not unfailing. It left us with wonderful memories, but it also left a hole. Only God's love never fails.

We are persecuted
but not abandoned; we
are struck down but not
destroyed. We always
carry the death of Jesus
in our body, so that the
life of Jesus may also be
revealed in our body.

2 Corinthians 4:9—10

The rejected person
who turns entirely to
God and His Word can
find glorious restoration
and acceptance in Christ
no matter what happens.
Whatever rejection you
have suffered, praying the
Scriptures can bring you
much strength.

He said to me,
"My grace is sufficient
for you, for power is
perfected in weakness."
Therefore, I will most
gladly boast all the more
about my weaknesses,
so that Christ's power
may reside in me.

2 Corinthians 12:9

Perhaps the success
of others has done little
more than increase your
discouragement. Don't let
the enemy play mind
games with you. God's
strength is tailor-made
for weakness. We are
never stronger than the
moment we admit
we are weak.

May the God of peace
Himself sanctify you
completely. And may your
spirit, soul, and body be
kept sound and blameless
for the coming of our
Lord Jesus Christ. He
who calls you is faithful,
who also will do it.

1 Thessalonians 5:23–24

God desires for us to
grant Him total access
to set apart every single
part of our lives—body,
soul, and spirit—to His
glorious work. Keep in
mind that anything to
God's glory is also
for our good.

Choose for yourselves today the one you will worship: the gods your fathers worshiped beyond the Euphrates River, or the gods of the Amorites in whose land you are living. As for me and my family, we will worship the Lord.

Joshua 24:15

Daily recommitments do not ensure that we will never fail, but they help us develop the mentality that every single day is a new day—a new chance to follow Christ.

The Spirit of the Lord
is on Me, because He has
anointed Me to preach
good news to the poor.
He has sent Me to
proclaim freedom to the
captives and recovery of
sight to the blind, to set
free the oppressed, to
proclaim the year of the
Lord's favor.

Luke 4:18—19

The moment we
admitted our guilt and
accepted our pardon, the
prison doors were opened.
And as much as Satan
wishes he held the keys
to lock them back again,
he doesn't. All he can do
is try to keep us seated
in an unlocked
prison cell.

I waited for sympathy,
but there was none; for
comforters, but found no
one. Instead, they gave
me gall for my food, and
for my thirst they gave
me vinegar to drink.

Psalm 69:20–21

While grief is
most assuredly not a
stronghold, lengthy
life-draining despair is.
Blocking the healing,
restorative power of
God places a believer
in a painful, literally
debilitating yoke
of bondage.

Do you not know that
your body is a sanctuary of
the Holy Spirit who is in
you, whom you have from
God? You are not your
own, for you were bought
at a price; therefore glorify
God in your body.

1 Corinthians 6:19 – 20

Since the Spirit of Christ dwells in the temple of believers' bodies, getting a Christian engaged in sexual sin is the closest Satan can ever come to personally assaulting Christ. That ought to make us mad enough to be determined to live victoriously.

Zacchaeus stood there and said to the Lord, "Look, I'll give half of my possessions to the poor, Lord! And if I have extorted anything from anyone, I'll pay back four times as much!"

Luke 19:8

Without exception, every
one of the overcomers
I know personally who
have come back to their
feet after terrible defeat
have lived in victory only
through a radical walk
with Jesus Christ
in truth.

Do not judge, so that
you won't be judged.
For with the judgment
you use, you will be
judged, and with the
measure you use, it will
be measured to you.

Matthew 7:1–2

We are wise not to judge others when they struggle to be free and seem to relapse over and over for a while. None of us is beyond facing the same challenge.

There is no one like You.
You are great; Your name
is great in power. Who
should not fear You, King
of the nations? It is what
You deserve. For among
all the wise people of the
nations and among all
their kingdoms, there
is no one like You.

Jeremiah 10:6—7

I think God must listen to our pitifully small acclamations and expectations of Him in prayer, and want to say, "Are you talking to Me? I'm not recognizing my-self in this conversation. Are you sure you have the right God?"

He demonstrated this power in the Messiah by raising Him from the dead and seating Him at His right hand in the heavens—far above every ruler and authority, power and dominion, and every title given, not only in this age but also in the one to come.

Ephesians 1:20—21

God applies the same
power to our need that
He exerted when He
raised Christ from the
dead. Does your need
require more power than
it takes to raise the dead?
Neither does mine. God
can do it, believer. I know
because He says so.

I do not consider
myself to have taken
hold of it. But one thing
I do: forgetting what is
behind and reaching
forward to what is ahead,
I pursue as my goal the
prize promised by God's
heavenly call in
Christ Jesus.

Philippians 3:13–14

There is abundant,
effective, Spirit-filled life
for those who are willing
to repent hard and work
hard. For folks like me,
there's not a lot of gray.
I learned the hard way
what can happen when
you wander too close to
a hole. You can fall in.

The salvation
and the power and the
kingdom of our God and
the authority of His
Messiah have now come,
because the accuser of our
brothers has been thrown
out: the one who accuses
them before our God
day and night.

Revelation 12:10

"You'll never be free. You've tried a hundred times. You always go back. You're hopeless. You're weak. You're a failure. You don't have what it takes." Every one of these statements about you is a lie if you're a believer in Christ.

Peter said, "Ananias, why has Satan filled your heart to lie to the Holy Spirit and keep back part of the proceeds from the field? . . . Why is it that you planned this thing in your heart? You have not lied to men but to God!"

Acts 5:3 – 4

Sometimes we're very aware of tolerating or even fueling a lie. Other times, we are caught in such a web that we can no longer see ourselves or our situation accurately. It is not always clear when we're being deceived, but one sure sign is when we too begin deceiving.

Pay attention to
the sound of my cry, my
King and my God, for I
pray to You. At daybreak,
Lord, You hear my voice;
at daybreak I plead my
case to You and watch
expectantly.

Psalm 5:2–3

What a heavy yoke
is shattered when we
awaken in the morning,
bring our hearts, minds,
and souls and all their
"needs" to the Great
Soul-ologist, offer Him
our empty cups, and
ask Him to fill them
with Himself.

As the Father has
loved me, I have also
loved you. Remain in
My love. If you keep
My commands you will
remain in My love, just as
I have kept My Father's
commands and remain
in His love.

John 15:9–10

Was it not the disciple
who reclined against
Jesus who saw himself as
the "beloved disciple"?
Place your ear against the
chest of the Savior so
that, when troubled times
come, you can hear the
steady pulse of His
boundless love.

When the goodness and
love for man appeared
from God our Savior, He
saved us—not by works of
righteousness that we had
done, but according to
His mercy, through the
washing of regeneration
and renewal by the
Holy Spirit.

Titus 3:4–5

Overcoming rejection is God's unquestionable will for your life. How do you do it? By applying large doses of God's love to your wounded heart daily and by allowing Him to renew your mind until the rejected thinks like the accepted.

The God of old is
your dwelling place,
and underneath are the
everlasting arms. He
drives out the enemy
before you, and
commands,
"Destroy!"

Deuteronomy 33:27

Begin to see yourself
like the young shepherd
boy David when he dared
to take a stand against
Goliath. What was the
key to David's courage?
He knew that Goliath was
not only *his* enemy. Far
more important, he
was *God's* enemy.

For the grace of God has
appeared, with salvation
for all people, instructing
us to deny godlessness
and worldly lusts and
to live in a sensible,
righteous, and godly
way in the present age.

Titus 2:11–12

Through the power
of the Holy Spirit and the
authority of His Word,
we are empowered to
say no to the things we
should—to our excesses,
compulsions, and harmful
consumptions—and to
say yes to freedom,
moderation, and
wholeness.

I am rejoicing, not
because you were grieved,
but because your grief led
to repentance. For you
were grieved as God
willed . . . For godly grief
produces a repentance
not to be regretted and
leading to salvation.

2 Corinthians 7:9 – 10

Godly sorrow
is not defined by tears
or outward displays of
contrition. Godly sorrow
is an authentic change
of heart resulting in
complete agreement
with God over
the matter.

To provide for those who mourn in Zion; to give them a crown of beauty instead of ashes, festive oil instead of mourning, and splendid clothes instead of despair. And they will be called righteous trees, planted by the Lord, to glorify Him.

Isaiah 61:3

Let God plunder
the enemy by bringing
so much good from the
bad, Satan will regret
ever taking us to the
wilderness of sin. What
divine vengeance occurs
when we let God use our
past failures to humble us,
refine us, and use us all
the more effectively.

When the devil had
finished all this tempting,
he left him until an
opportune time.

Luke 4:13 NIV

Satan is an opportunist.
Would he come after you
while you are down?
In a heartbeat,
if he had a heart.

Where can I go from
your Spirit? Where can
I flee from your presence?
If I go up to the heavens,
you are there; if I make
my bed in the depths,
you are there.

Psalm 139:7–8 NIV

We often see ourselves
as fragile, breakable souls.
But actually, only our
pride is fragile. Once its
shell is broken and the
heart is laid bare, we can
sense the caress of God's
tender care. Until then,
He holds us just the same.

So also the Messiah,
having been offered once
to bear the sins of many,
will appear a second time,
not to bear sin, but to
bring salvation to those
who are waiting for Him.

Hebrews 9:28

Have you waited long upon the Lord? For His Word? For His hand? Until He speaks and acts, and He surely will, you need not wait upon His love. Patience to wait does not come from suffering long for what we lack but from sitting long in what we have.

I will not restrain my mouth. I will speak in the anguish of my spirit; I will complain in the bitterness of my soul.

Job 7:11

Intimacy with God
means sharing the depths
of our hearts with Him.
If what is in the depths is
great joy and celebration,
then share it with Him.
And if what is in the
depths is anger, hurt,
and all sorts of injury,
tell Him that too!

How much more will
the blood of the Messiah,
who through the eternal
Spirit offered Himself
without blemish to God,
cleanse our consciences
from dead works to
serve the living God?

Hebrews 9:14

The reason we keep going
back to our strongholds is
that we have temporarily
been delivered from the
sin practice, but we did
not follow through with
deliverance to the healthy
heart of God. The key to
deliverance is not being
delivered *from* but being
delivered *to*.

Test me, Lord,
and try me; examine
my heart and mind.
For Your faithful love
is before my eyes, and
I live by Your truth.

Psalm 26:2 – 3

What is my revenge
after all the devil has done
to me? To let God make
me twice the foe of hell
I would ever have been
otherwise. What is my
joy? Walking in truth, so
aware of where I've been
that I cleave to Christ
Jesus like a sash around
His priestly robe.

Teach me Your way,
Lord, and I will live by
Your truth. Give me an
undivided mind to fear
Your name. I will praise
You with all my heart,
Lord my God, and will
honor Your name
forever.

Psalm 86:11 – 12

You and I as believers in
Christ have been chosen
to know and understand
that He is God and there
is no other. And yet this
very One is our Father,
who both demands and
deserves our respect.
Without it, for all
practical purposes,
we are powerless.

Therefore let us approach the throne of grace with boldness, so that we may receive mercy and find grace to help us at the proper time.

Hebrews 4:16

How do you find the throne of grace in your time of need? Follow the blood drops! Then come as boldly as you possibly can. The praying man is the one heaven sees with bloodstains on his knees.

If you have faith
the size of a mustard
seed, you will tell this
mountain, "Move from
here to there," and it will
move. Nothing will be
impossible for you.

Matthew 17:20

Once again today,
God has a will for your
life, Christ has a Word
for your life, and the
Holy Spirit has a way
for your life. Nothing
is impossible.

If I, your Lord and
Teacher, have washed
your feet, you also ought
to wash one another's
feet. For I have given
you an example that you
also should do just as
I have done for you.

John 13:14–15

Christ could afford to be humble as He served upon this earth. After all, He was the Son of God. He had nothing to prove. And as joint heirs with Christ, neither do we. So go wash a few feet. God's most liberated servants are those who know they have nothing to prove.

Where envy and selfish
ambition exist, there is
disorder and every kind
of evil. But the wisdom
from above is first pure,
then peace-loving, gentle,
compliant, full of mercy
and good fruits, without
favoritism and hypocrisy.

James 3:16–17

Under conviction of
worldliness, many well-
meaning persons have
simply transferred their
huge egos from the world
to the church. Beware of
spiritual ambition. We are
most useful to God when
poured free of self and
full of Christ.

Do you not know
that friendship with the
world is hostility toward
God? So whoever wants
to be the world's friend
becomes God's enemy.

James 4:4

In our search for unfailing
love, if we unknowingly
allow Satan to become
our tour guide, our quest
will undoubtedly lead
to captivity.

Are you so foolish? After beginning with the Spirit, are you now going to be made complete by the flesh?

Galatians 3:3

Believe what God's
Word tells you about
Him and about you. You
are defined by the love
and acceptance of the
Creator and Sustainer
of the universe.

We had natural fathers
discipline us, and we
respected them. Shouldn't
we submit even more to
the Father of spirits and
live? For they disciplined
us for a short time based
on what seemed good to
them, but He does it for
our benefit, so that we
can share His holiness.

Hebrews 12:9–10

God is never unbiased
toward His children. He
does not momentarily set
aside His parenthood to
discipline us objectively
and unaffectionately. He
never parts the sea of His
fathomless love to take us
across begrudgingly.

He predestined us
to be adopted through
Jesus Christ for Himself,
according to His favor
and will, to the praise of
His glorious grace that
He favored us with
in the Beloved.

Ephesians 1:5–6

God was pleased to
make you His own.
Pleased! He didn't just
feel sorry for you. He
wasn't obligated to you.
He chose you because
He delights in you.

Even my friend in whom
I trusted, one who ate my
bread, has lifted up his
heel against me. But You,
Lord, be gracious to me
and raise me up.

Psalm 41:9 – 10

Our lives are steeped in
constant change. Fingers
are painfully peeled away
from the security of
sameness one at a time.
With hands freshly
loosed, we find liberty to
embrace the One who
will never change, and
courage to release to Him
those who ever will.

For the Lord your
God is gracious and
merciful; He will not
turn His face away
from you if you
return to Him.

2 Chronicles 30:9

Be tenacious and
patient, child of God. If
you fall, don't listen to the
accusations and jeers of
the evil one. Get back up
and walk with God again.
How many times?
Until you're free.

Above all,
put on love—the
perfect bond of unity.
And let the peace of
the Messiah, to which
you were also called in
one body, control
your hearts.

Colossians 3:14–15

I know far too well how
distant the peace of God
is when we refuse to bow
a part of our lives to His
rule. Peace is the fruit of
authority. *God's* authority.
Christ brings His peace
where He is Prince.

If the Lord had not
been my help, I would
soon rest in the silence
of death. If I say, "My foot
is slipping," Your faithful
love will support
me, Lord.

Psalm 94:17—18

None of us can master ourselves. God is the only One who can sanctify and make every part of us whole. All He wants is our trust, our belief, and a little time.

Wash away my guilt, and
cleanse me from my sin.
For I am conscious of my
rebellion, and my sin is
always before me. Against
You—You alone—I have
sinned and done this evil
in Your sight. So You
are right when You
pass sentence.

Psalm 51:2–4

One reliable rod for
measuring closeness to
God would be the time
that lapses between sin
and repentance. This
overwhelming sensitivity
results in a holier life
because you repent in
the early stages of what
otherwise would become
a contagion of sin.

Do not repay evil
with evil or insult with
insult, but with blessing,
because to this you were
called so that you may
inherit a blessing.

1 Peter 3:9 NIV

God created our hearts
so uniquely that they are
forced to forgive in order
to be free. He greatly
honors our willingness
to bless others when our
human reaction would
be to curse them.

Joshua told the people,
"Consecrate yourselves,
because the Lord will
do wonders among
you tomorrow."

All believers have
been set apart from the
unclean to the clean, from
the unholy to the holy.
And when believers act
like the sanctified people
they are, God is released
to do powerful wonders
among them.

This is why you must
take up the full armor
of God, so that you may
be able to resist in the evil
day, and having prepared
everything, to take
your stand.

Ephesians 6:13

A war of unprecedented proportions is waging against the church and the people of God. We must put on our armor, learn how to use our weapons, and fight with the confidence of those who know they are destined to win.

As for me, I will never boast about anything except the cross of our Lord Jesus Christ, through whom the world has been crucified to me, and I to the world.

Galatians 6:14

Give much time and thought to becoming well-equipped victors in the battle that rages, but give *more* time to your pursuit of the heart of God and all things concerning Him. Much about warfare. More about God Himself.